This **Mermaid's** Coloring book belongs to

. . . .

You can start
from here

Images: Freepik.com

INSTAGRAM

nini_publisher

Visit our instagram, share your opinion on amazon about this coloring book. You can also share your artworks!

Thanks for your buying !!